Something

P.J. KAVANAGH was born in England ⸺, ⸺ ⸺ worked as a lecturer, actor and broadcaster, as well as a writer. His *Collected Poems* were published in 1992, the year in which he was given the Cholmondely Award for poetry. His memoir *The Perfect Stranger* won the Richard Hillary Prize in 1966, and his first novel *A Song and Dance* was awarded the Guardian Fiction Prize in 1968. From 1983 to 1996 P.J. Kavanagh was a columnist on the *The Spectator*, and from 1996 to 2002 on *The Times Literary Supplement*. In addition to his four novels for adults and two children's novels, he has written a travel autobiography (*Finding Connections*), a literary companion (*Voices in Ireland*) and has edited *The Oxford Book of Short Poems* and *The Essential G.K. Chesterton*, and, for Carcanet, a new edition of his *Collected Poems of Ivor Gurney*. P.J. Kavanagh lives in Gloucestershire.

P.J. KAVANAGH

Something About

CARCANET

Acknowledgements

A number of these poems have appeared in *The Rialto*, *Cyphers*, *The Spectator*, *PN Review*, and *The Times Literary Supplement*.

For Michael Schmidt

First published in Great Britain in 2004 by
Carcanet Press Limited
Alliance House
Cross Street
Manchester M2 7AQ

A CIP catalogue record for this book is available from the British Library
ISBN 1 85754 646 6

The publisher acknowledges financial assistance from Arts Council England

Typeset in Bembo by XL Publishing Services
Printed and bound in England by SRP Ltd, Exeter

Contents

Occasionals

Beside the sea

Was it the blouse-and-skirt combination, the cut
Of the fair hair of the near-silhouette
Against shining sea, that made me peer and stare?
I screwed up my eyes, unfocused, to see less clear
And keep you a moment longer, hold you there.
It has happened before, of course, as though round a corner
Impossible things may appear. A middle-aged woman
I saw when I secretly led us to where
I could see with my back to the sea, who had nothing in common
With you save stature and stoop and short-cut yellow hair.
We moved on. Not self nor pain nor fate is here nor there,
But relentlessly turns us to souls that peer and stare.

The new man

Cricket captains cry on television – even Australian.
'I love you' is commonplace now, to hesitate is repression.
'Love you', child's cellphone sign-off, parent and son.
In the crowded cathedral at mid-Mass handshake Sign
of Peace, 'I love ya, Patrick!' (my name) made me turn,
startled: a bearded American hugged his male companion.

Do I say it, ever? Perhaps, but insufficiently often,
doubtless from prudence, or fear; something about Temptation
of Providence, plus the old idea, 'Actions speak louder than…'
Only after one suddenly died, in outraged indignation
did I bawl, 'But I loved you!' as though we'd been
hardly done by. Too late now. It was a shared hesitation.
Though I would have enjoyed a Bronx cheer from you, a comedian-
beauty, your pleased, teasing derision. Different then.

Autumn

Hurry, the morning's going,
Though barely it clears cross-bars
Of telegraph-poles, their wires
Dew-wet, are dripping light.
Soon, buried in briars,
We'll have to hack for it.

Rooks are sounding thawed,
Grasses crackle, proud
They have survived the night.
An after-breakfast match-flame
Vanishes, sun-blasted,
On the blackened stick.

Like flocks of birds our souls
Have many things, and separate,
To settle on and eat.
Now creosoted poles –
Light on their wires gone out –
Black sticks and disconnected.
It is always late.

Slow as grass

I'm growing patience as the cut grass grows
Blunt-headed, stubborn, in a warm November,
Blunt where cut to last all winter but it grows
On, blunt-headed. I am not yet patient as the grass,
Waiting the melt of mist that soaked it flat
Splashed by the feet of cattle into suns,
Hoof-high. As the sun climbs the day dries.

Now elephant cloud-teams drag behind them grey
Tarpaulin, evening. Riding it come children
Last seen trailing (like dressing-gown cords) their dreams.
At dusk I hurl a ball with them, still waiting,
Pretending a day complete which is only ending,
Growing to patience as they will have to grow
Or mimic what seems day's busyness, but day
Is never busy, is as slow as grass.

Cat, budgerigar, and answer

It seems, old fat cat, likely
that you will die before me
(nothing is certain) and I'd like to think
you'd take a small portion of love I have given
your gentleness over the years
(not a scratch, only sheathed warning-punches in fifteen)
to brush, unexpected, purring, round the legs
of her I would like to receive that love, and you.
A surprise, in short, from elsewhere,
sent from me (which is a way
of thinking. Nothing is certain).
Good it would be if it worked the other way
and we were sometimes brushed…

Warm and dry it alights, almost weightlessly, and
as light and dry as this trusting bird on my finger
the weight of a hand curved round the back of my hand
I suddenly remember.

November

I am almost too snobbish to mention the commonplace bird,
Elusive as insight, each in the dark of its tree,
Which stitches these dawns and these sunsets with needling phrases
Till beginnings and endings of days seem coloured, embroidered.
Secretive birds; now in full light of day
They flit within shadow, and watch from there, silently,
As though they consider for shortening days short praises
Sufficient, or insult enough to keep their rivals at bay.

Sacred, not sentimental; if a man who is lying in bed
Is seeing competitive birdsong as coloured thread,
When you know it the sound of the season and time of the day,
Let him. Allow him his human compulsion to say –
Whatever the reason the birds have for briefly singing –
Two robins embroidered this morning and may do this evening.

Angels

If I knew what they wished me to say I would say it.
If I knew the right prayer for my case I would pray it.
Would you have me bear witness on knees in the street
Like Christopher Smart? 'I'd as lief pray with Kit
Smart as with anyone else,' grunts the Great Cham,
But those days are gone, and the words to affirm.
If you set me a dangerous task I would do it
(I hope), or your hoop, I would try to jump through it.

These are angels, not devils, I know, that beset me,
Elusive as rainbows the problems they set me.
Their wings are the rainbows that beckon me on,
To hear what I cannot hear, quite. They are stern:
'Write it down, what we tell you!' 'What? Please say it again!'

Like swallows they gathered, like swallows are gone.

Tug o' war

It does not become a gentleman so to go on
About *anything*; he should smile. His burden
(Or his refrain), his continual 'Where is it?'
Will make the company yawn, the audience fidget.
As Painted Ladies or Peacocks he should be light
On the buddleia flower, as brief and as delicate.
But, unencumbered by manners, the tug of his search is so desperate,
Poor baffled creature, he feels he has to share it.

Will you turn the rope on your wrist and make him your anchor
                                                    man?
He hasn't the bulk now, obsession has hollowed him out.
Perhaps you prefer him in front of you, taking this strain
He seems to be feeling, although you can feel none?
And he goes on, pulling at air, smelling of sweat.
'At least,' he is grunting, 'I'm not a gentleman.'

A gottle o' Guinness

Should a man catch a glimpse of the feet of the shapes
That exist beyond eyeshot, he knows he must follow, though songs
Swirl in him, soundless, because he wearily knows,
Or is told, his times mistrust brightnesses, choose
Deconstruction; they clamp his tongue in tongs.
Still he moves in the draught of their movement – the feet
Grow into logic, have ankles and shins and kneecaps
With faces above – though he seldom dares lift up his eyes.

Such a man cannot, an old-fashioned Music Hall 'vent',
Become his own dummy, choose only pronounceable phrases
Consonant with his times, or allow them to work his dissident
Mouth, with their hands up his jacket,
Or keep a still face, forced to say, 'It is nonsense perhaps'.
His tongue and his palate betray him. Watch his lips.

A memory

Lost along a nightlane above the sea at Falmouth,
An only light, an empty fish and chip shop
Cool as a green cave. Gleaming walls
Like Italian water-ices, coloured sorbets,
Nut-green, a line, pale lemon. A daughter
Smiling, a sharper mother, smiling.
Salt, vinegar. 'Here, keep you going!'
Below, we had talked of art, or magic – foundering.
Alone, now here it was! Why should shine
So thin a place, and two smiles?
Between blank walls without a picture, not
A calendar? Torn neatly, skewered newspapers.
I looked. 'They're old.' They were. The top, of all
Dates, your far birthdate! Of all times,
Of all places, lost along a nightlane, such a shine.

Mood indigo, tune Irish

When frogs begin croaking and winter's long soaking
    today's sun is stroking up into white mist
with small birds inside it, we cannot avoid it,
    we ought to insist it is good to exist.

Though birds in their twinning can hardly be sinning
    now springtime is winning its race to begin,
the truth is I call to white mist the hawk falls through
    as though my soul begs of it 'Please let me in!'

O, a need to be vaporous, blanker than paper is
    sometimes possesses us till we cry out
'Off, off you leavings, you woundings, bereavings,
    and our self-deceivings (the worst of the lot)!'

This hasn't occurred to you? Here is my word to you:
    Christ in his mercy may give you the call…
Or turn with a frown to you, looking right down in you,
    wonder – *By thunder, where were you at all?*

After Westwell churchyard

When faith and likelihood collide
you hear no sound, you're looking at a screen
gone suddenly blank, your computer's down
and years and memories lie coiled inside
unblinking uninforming green.

You feel you've gone transparent, like those fish
which, heads against the current, flick and strain.
Your self drained colourless, your self as seen
in a photograph captioned 'A blankminded man
outside a pub beside the Windrush.'

Two talking friends, loved women, briefly gone
to view another church, I'm left alone
to work out on a broken-down machine
(and with this fishlike sense of waking sleep)
what we thought when standing by the stone

which marked the grave of someone we had known
in our three different ways. Those ways devout,
all three believers; who believed in what?
All four of us would one day meet again?
Collision. Likelihood gone ploughing into hope

and sweetness drained away. My emptied mind
so swept and garnished devils might fly in.
My prayer was (and Blankman bends his knees)
not to be too far tested. Please. Please.
Most needful of our prayers, from the gut.

Returning, my companions see no change.
None there to see, this is inside-weather
but change is needful, weathers play their part
in growth, in learning and in just decay.
No answer comes from staring at a grave.

Fish strain and feed, and we go off together,
to strain to see the living as they are:
bewildered, needy and (we must be) brave
when what we know we need seems out of range.

'Constancy to an ideal object'

S.T. Coleridge

'Reaching right through inside
the curtain' (Isaiah) – 'all
things counterfeit infinity'
(S.T.C.) – under our hand,
gloved by darkness,
all stills, thrills, at a power,
powerful, we feel, precisely
because it is not underhand.

'The best, the truly lovely
in each & all is God.
Therefore the truly Beloved
is the symbol of God.'
And not idolatry?
Though easy to love an absence...
As in his poem wonder-filled
Coleridge wondered, in the end.

Because of a glimpse of Heaven
manifest, briefly unburied,
revealed in the roots of our clay,
which I knew was doubly intended
– our visible world is a grave
pun, I never doubted
we live in a serious joke –
but did we honey in lap-land?

Today bright fieldfares come
to make our hedges bend,
this is their berried heaven, after Lapland...
I dreamed of a gold-crested wren,
its punk yellow hair-streak
turning to dust on my thumb –
gold, still, at the down-roots.

Not all comes away in the hand.

Ascension window at Fairford

for Colette Clark

'Things are the Sons of Heaven'
growled Samuel Johnson...

But oh, we tire of clay
which binds us, of the way –
(with bolts of bones, that fettered stands
in feet, and manacled in hands) –
our flesh makes soul absurd.

Then we remember Fairford
where in coloured glass we saw a crowd,
tethered in boots, stare up at a cloud
as though to hitch a ride,
but could not, they were tied
to earth, like us, as Henry Vaughan complained.
Thus tied, we look up too and understand
what they are marvelling at;
the soles of two bare feet
stick downwards from the bottom of the cloud.

Feet are what slacken the jaws of the fleshly crowd,
were Things, could be defined,
not Abstracts (which the mind
prefers to hide inside) plain as the nose
on your face, and why the artist shows

Christ entering the Cosmos
showing his ten toes.

Whitsun

At times you can watch a sheep almost shaping a thought,
Mid-grazing it raises its head then takes a few steps,
Stops, head erect, blank-eyed and clearly thinking.
Until, with no shrug, it surrenders and goes back to eating,
What nearly formed in its skull is this time abandoned.
(As we might climb upstairs in search of something,
Forget, stand puzzled, and come down empty-handed.)

An exceptional blackbird, Caruso, sings from mid-sag
Of the house-wire (his favourite platform) a perfect cadenza:
Replied to, note for note, by another blackbird.
Human, you think, 'competition – Caruso will blast him
New grace-notes so complex he cannot match them'. Silence.
You turn: has abandoned his platform. Is not human.
(One aria blew his foe from his bush, he scuttled beneath it.)

Match drawn. It feels we are here on earth to watch creation –
Do you not think so? – it seems like our diet, our feeding.
Nourishment not apprehended, not quite, a grazing
Elsewhere, unpuzzled and grateful, in no way thinking.
Something come down from somewhere, as we have to come
                                                    down also
(A sheep, two blackbirds, none of them where we last saw them)
With nothing at all in our hands – and not empty-handed.

Vox Pop

'To be fair', 'to be perfectly honest' – such otiose phrases recur
In interviews, sports-reports, radio phone-ins, the air
Is moted with such talking-tics, till I shout at the set
'*Why be anything else!*' But under the rubbish that dribbles from
                                                            every mouth
You hear an unconscious homage to what we most care about –
So rare we have almost forgotten them – Justice, Mercy, Truth.

Small voice

Yesterday a gusting wind made float
flat deer-shapes over the surface of green wheat,
today it is twitching shoals of silver fish
which at the field's sky-edge are white
gulls in flocks, they fly and never take off.

Nothing is there, not gulls nor fish nor deer,
nothing but moving air and the voice we hear
is not in the wind and what we say we feel
about what we see and we nearly hear will not
(which is good) be ever quite right or enough.

Seasonal

1

Summer: a three-headed bird – white
Kestrel fledglings wedged so tight together,
Are triune on the barn-attic sill.
They browned and flew and on the day
Came families of rooks to buzz them.
One falcon, first time borne by air
Dived headlong into ashtree mattress, and
A junior rook, head-cocked, peeped in
The bathroom window – 'See? We showed 'em!'

2

Combine-harvesters: their massive matings
With lascivious tractor-trailers
Which wriggle, the better to take their seed.
Stubble: lion-flanks with yellow
Highlights, straw in shining lines,
And rooks again, black on the curving streaks
Of gold, prospecting: baled to ingots
Red tractors tidy, play chess with, on the lion's side.
Then harrow, harrow, fur become brown tweed.

3

Rain: and leaf-choked gutters stain the ceiling.
A climb to clear them, eyes expecting
Greyness. No, a bonsai garden!
Fra Angelico flowerets, emerald
Moss, to lift off with a finger. No.
Too innocent. Too perfect. Too content.
Leave them undisturbed, unharvested,
Too much the world is rudely shaken…

Later, pale-faced hogweed nods defiant
Of cold wind, each side the lane,
Insists it still is autumn. We drive between
Them, grateful. We are shaken
By flux of season, too much change.
Today we learned what had been left alone
Generation to generation
Said to have belonged to Thomas More
In the Abbey from its pedestal torn
The bronze Prinknash Virgin has been stolen.

What I didn't say to Thomas

1

Your frayed and tweeded arm
pointed up to Heaven:
'You still believe in Him?'
Interested, kindly.
Evasive my reply:
'Nuns got me early.'
It is glimpses stop me dead
(I should have said):
An orange shop-front blurred
by a bus's passing red;
the swoop of a grounded bird
I had thought was wounded,
to the top of a misty tree.

Such glimpses have no Future,
no Present either,
only a past, it is always
'*Then* there is one' –
not *was* because no longer
than love or a piece of string
glimpses have power
to linger, to throw open
an unexpected door
(hand kept on the latch, a curator's gesture)
and the twitchy visitor stopped dead by wonder.

2

There is always a contradiction
which seems like a confirmation:
there comes into the mind – no Visitation –
a smiling visitor. Huge charm,
a winning way long out of fashion
(perhaps I can't outface a fresher one)
he seems the witty, camper kind of don;
his quick perception and his bubbling jokes
enchantingly much quicker than my own,
who pouts at me and looks at what I see
and – Pouf! – he nearly blows it all away.
I falter (he is fun) but must insist, 'I'll never –'
he quickly turns and frowns, 'My dear,
never say never!'
                    Serious at last.
It sounds his creed.
                    'However,
time I suppose to *seem* to disappear.'
He leaves a whiff of bay-rum on the air…

3

Thomas, such misty confusion
(which is not always one)
I should have dared to drop on
your sceptical head, historian,
the morning we walked from Elkstone,
and you teasingly asked your question,
past the place where an un-
wounded owl swept both it and me
high to a misty tree.

I know I shirked a duty
with 'Nuns got me early.'

27

Two syllabics

Thank God for syllables, they allow you to say
Significant trivials, included no other way.
For this I thank Roy Fuller's, Marianne Moore's and Auden's.
All other forms, at times, can be censoring Wardens.

1. Christmas walk

Alone: its qualities are light
(A growing dusk) and this almost holy silence.
    Diminishing light increases,
Intensifies, how lichened tree-trunks glow, and green-
    Finches going black in hedges
Sky-framed. Just-built and newly abandoned (farmers
    Go bust; ask them why, you'll get mum
For no answer), a breeze-block dairy, odorous
    Centre of lowing, clanking life,
Now part of silence. Rubber tubes, black, with shining
    Silver nozzles patiently hang,
Expectant. A rat has thrown up a mound of new
    Soil from a crack in the guano-
Encrusted concrete, from twenty-one refugee
    Racing pigeons. A mystery,
Carefully counted because their number a fact
    And facts as hard to come by
As explanations – Sellotaped to the milk-tank
    A graph of milk-production,
Going *up*. Built ten years ago and now so gone
    It could be Anglo-Saxon.
Moving on, lane gliding under the feet, as thoughts
    Glide through the head, forgotten
As soon as thought, going somewhere; unrecorded,
    Description is false without them,
But tedious when recycled. Trust the picture.
    Horizoned, a silhouette
With a see-saw limp, against a reddening sky,
    Is scattering hay for cattle,
Tearing his tight-packed bale into giant biscuits
    Impatiently skimmed, quoited. Slow
And dignified, black and white heifers (limping man

Scoots off), slow, from the farthest corner
Of their darkening theatre, moving like gentle
        Gunslingers – first one shoulder
Then the other – stroll towards their Yule-tide handsel,
        Embodied silence, going dark.

2. Test Match Special

Insufficiently reflective, or too
Self-indulgent, to believe my dead are
        Genuinely gone,
Like many another subconsciously
Hoping a hinting arrival – *not*
        'Communication'
(Lusting too hotly for visitation
Presumes too much, it can arrive but none
        By willing is won).

This world's horrors acknowledged, one-day
More heavy, leadened, by weight of man's
        Swinishness to man –
Though fairly unguilty – my day's duties,
Or so I assure myself doubtfully,
        Seem dusted and done –
I lie by a butterfly-buddleia
Some bird-scaring field-glasses near me, with
        The radio on,

And half-hear a Test Match (field-glasses are
Prophylactic for birds; hung round your neck
        You'll never see one).
Through soft-falling chat – what, has the Holy
Spirit decided to show I am wrong?
        What an occasion
Would that be! – binoculars grabbed in time,
So close it could be standing on my thumb,
        Descends this bird.

Not even bending the shoot it lands on,
Warbler-stranger too yellow for England,
        Less weight than a word.
Black-eyeliner-elegant, legs twig-grey,
Preening, milk-white under sorbet-yellow,
        Clearly considered
Cricket-talk reassuring – which it is.
As far apart as closest lovers are
        Our shade is shared.

★

'Melodious Warbler,' looked up later,
'Common in France.' In English the name sounds
        Prissily absurd,
But not the bird, its beauty. *Hippolais*
Polyglotta, our lust for facts insists
        As insist it should,
Up to a point. But this was past that point.
This was enough. Weightless it might have seemed,
        But part of the Word.
'Song distinctive, faster, less discordant
Than the Ictyrine.' A confirmation –
        If it had been heard.

Properly discreet our visitations
Hint us enough; from this one in August
        Not a dicky-bird.

Dawns

Seated majestic slant-eyed painted Siena
Madonnas float in a 'habitable ether'.
'God so loved the world...' he made it easy for

himself with dawn-colours, Gurney's 'rose-on-thorn'
here, sun biting a chunk from the pyloned horizon
briefly, then healing it, world spinning on

until – the changes imperceptible –
pink sky-trails fade to palest daffodil
and all Pen Hill's ablaze, a moment's beacon-hill,

but roads stay gilded, pylons, dew-wet sheep,
a gilt-edged invitation we escape
by sleeping through mid-winter curtain-up.

'But "a habitable ether" needs some *rigour*'
you insist? Well, mother and child, Madonna
after Madonna, seem never to puncture

Duccio's semi-dream, his wholly fact. True,
his world half-waked when young Giotto
painted Lazarus in his grave-clothes, held by two –

one vomits, other, cloth to mouth and nose.
But before that, long before that, in another place
('A bad smell mixed with glory' remembered MacNeice

of Ravenna) a Maecenas must have decided, 'Maestro,
do us a Transfiguration!' Squares of clay and glue,
colour (and bad smell) what did some genius do

impossibly commanded? What's to be seen
fifteen centuries on? An apse; half-bowl of green
and on it a queue of sheep, backs gilt by dawn,

white flowers in between them, simplified
rocks, shrubs, trees. A dawn world-wide
made wider by an empty cross of brown, inside

which, tiny, out of eye-reach, like a brooch,
is set Christ's puzzled face. No more than that.
And a small hand pointing down at him. Such
rigour, dawn-simplicity, knocks you flat.

Something about

those huge black canvases in Newman's
church, St Stephen's Green – restoration
botched perhaps – Raphael Cartoons,
copies, loved by Newman, quite gone out.
      Something about,
outside, Joyce's head, too silver-sharp,
too shrunk, facing stone steps he argued up
of the house where Hopkins sweated, found his heart,
his shaping spirit, turned 'widow of an insight
lost' (which we know something about).
      Something about
a pigeon-flight above the little lake, dark then white
as they turn as one bird and repeat
black into white (as ruined paint will not)
nine times precisely and like one bird depart.
      Strange the fate –
insight spoiled, wanting rhymes too neat,
whichever way we think, wherever look –
to snuffle like setters in a winter garden
excitedly nosing old leaves, mortally certain
there is (certainly was – night's odorous traffic)
      something, somewhere, about.

Gold

Her voice: 'Tell me about it, growing old.'
   His: 'On cold mornings your nose goes red, your eyes
so full of rheum you blink and see the world

refracted, gold. (Other indignities,
   leaden to mention, grant a bleaker prospect.)
But eyes you look through, strangely, stay a boy's,

so only guess your change from brusque respect,
   impatient eyes of those with time
gold in the bank, to whom you are an abstract

not to be kissed. Maybe we climb
   up, away and through those eyes to a half-
remembered, half-believed-in Golden Clime – '

Her voice: 'At times your nose was red. It made me laugh.'
   His: ' – which is surely self-deception? Mm? The gold
talc of your laugh is still on my skin, a graph

up to the possible. Laughter I had, but yours, unwilled
   unconscious and instinctive, was your gift,
plugged to a larger, never a smaller, world,

confirming what I hoped for – that every rift
   could be loaded with ore, with awe – language was there
to be played with, sailed with, till we could drift

into glimmer and glow, could Fred Astaire
   it, coral lagoons for dance-floors, pray and play and – '
Her voice: ' – pay?' His: 'A high price. Old and baffled, to peer
                            and stare,

gold turned marsh-mist which we can't see through,
   and yellow fog-damp muffling, we can't hear.'
Hers: 'You may not see, but hear you can and do...'

(But can I believe a voice in my head? Although
   when did I ever doubt it?) 'So, there comes relief?'
Her voice: 'Not yet. Never, maybe. I don't know.'

Whichever voice said that a golden leaf
teased and see-sawed, spinning slowly down,
autumn it was, then more came, in a drift.
Some tree, deep-rooted? No, a sacred stone,
a sarsen, plugged so deep no man can shift.

His voice: 'Don't ever believe (I don't) my disbelief.'

London Bridge

A thruppenny bunch of violets bought from a hawker,
A gypsy-woman in long foreign skirts, and there
Were decided two young lives, once and for all.
And there were staked the heads of Saint Thomas More
And Saint John Fisher, 'which daily grew fresher and fresher'
(The latter), 'in his lifetime he never looked so well',
And crowds came to gawp, so his head was thrown in the water.
More's head was bought by his daughter, Margaret Roper,
Before it was thrown in the Thames; further
Room being required, for further heads. And sunken St Saviour,
Southwark Cathedral, hugged by the railway viaduct, tolls its bell
Over the graves of Gower, and Edmund, Shakespeare's brother,
And grace-filled Lancelot Andrewes. Ghosts crowd this quarter.

Catholics, Protestants, others, died for a serious matter,
Serious to them, still is, because they were sincere.
And neat in suits, overflowing the pavement, young from Pakistan
Are cheering their cricketers on, against India, street television,
Close to The Tabard. And pilgrims of genial Chaucer
Started from here; and someone has written, each white letter
Symmetrical, perfect, on soot-stained brick: I KNOW I HAVE
                                                          LOST –
Such a cry – two streets away, on the back of a rotting warehouse.

One who seeks a particular ghost –
A thruppenny bunch of violets bought from a hawker
And two young lives decided for good and always –
Asks if such a private haunting matters? Knows it does,
When he sees it, watching him, join hands with every other.

Job

I am not at ease, neither am I quiet, neither have I rest.

Who lives in the eye of love is not alone.
But think of his burden! Closed-circuit surveillance.
'Not long enough for me to swallow my spittle'
is ever the lens turned away, nor can he guess
what monsters swim in him blithely, and unknown.
Still, his God subdued the Great Sea Beast, peers down
on sea and him, while swifter than a weaver's shuttle
his days clank on. 'Am I the Sea or the Great Sea Beast
that you should keep me under watch and guard?'
An image not from Freud but Babylon –
comfort, perhaps, the longevity of that question.

But creeping things and birds and fish and cattle,
our earth companions, 'not one such creature but has known
this state of things is all of God's own making.
A man becomes a laughing-stock to his friends
if he cries to God and expects an answer!' One
who knows by heart the lesson learns again
the Deal: you live in the eye of love, and on your own.

Occasionals

For Wogan's seventy-fifth birthday, 1978

*Poems should not need introductions but with Occasional ones they can help.
These lines, resurrected because I still agree with them – the ideas that the serious
should be treated lightly, and that we seldom make decisions, they make us – were
written for my dear father-in-law Wogan Philipps and I was mildly surprised at
how coolly he received them. Now I see that to him, devout Communist, soldier in
the cause of willed progress, both notions would have been heretical – as well as
loopy.*

In nineteen fifty-four
– Or was it fifty-three?
(Your anniversary
Is so grave a matter
I must take it lightly)
I came here with your daughter.

So long a visit ought
Explain why it was stayed.
Are all decisions *made*?
You may think it so.
I know and do not know.
I think I stayed because I did not go.

A day of New Year snow
In nineteen fifty-three
(Or was it fifty-four?)
Has so long stayed with me
It may never melt.
We feel what we have felt.

I learn the lanes you knew
Before I even saw,
Still see them in the snow
I saw with her and you,
And I am grateful for
A first day that was new
As you were then, and are.

'Cock Robin'

for Charles Causley

This happened: Causley, arrived from Cornwall, trapped in a car with a gaggle of poets, recited the whole – vast – ballad of 'Cock Robin'. It was a defensive joke, of course, but it also seemed to contain an invitation, to enter his world, or take it or leave it.

Once upon a time, I wrote with my hat on,
and scarfed, as though against snow.
Perhaps I thought the hat would keep my thoughts in.
Anyway, I was dressed ready to get up and go.

Then one came jauntily riding out of the West,
watchfully friendly, like an old gunslinger
who under his duffle-coat wore an armoured vest,
who shot all enquiries dead by reciting a

lengthy MS of 'Cock Robin' until he had set
about ninety-nine verses into a parapet
he could peer through with safety and then ride out
of range – 'Like my hat!'

I called after him. 'You have a thought to keep in,
and you hide it in jokes and rhymes I cannot quite
laugh at in comfort, and that is right!
Like a sentry you guard it and it makes you sing!'

(Only the sound of pain is worth the listening,
but no complaint of pain is worth a straw.
You told us nothing that we need not know.)
But it's not so bad, a wilderness of two.

Heartened, I looked up at last and saw
outside my room was miles of frozen snow.
Not trackless, now. I was dressed ready to get up and go.

Toronto Poetry Festival

for Peter Levi

'Your business in this city?'
'To read our poetry.'
Absurd… and Immigration
Now talks to us in German.

Banks like Peloponnesian
Mani towers in competition,
Like San Gimigniano even.
One is carated golden.

In scabbards our ambition,
Careful our conversation,
Gathered together, convention
Of mother-of-pearl salesmen.

★

Beneath such competition,
Behind those orgulous towers,
Low-built by refugees
From unforgotten Famine

Is Irish 'Cabbage Town'
Which keeps a farm for children.
There's been a dispossession.
The manger of a golden

Calf a portly rabbit occupies,
With eyes become Chinese
In sleep, as long as heron
Wings its folded ears,

It couches on the manger's iron bars.
Calf gently lips what green
That oriental doze
And rabbit-bulk allows

To dangle from above.
Pulls single blades of grass,
Fears to erect flat ears,
Make round those Chinese eyes.

It seems a form of love,
Reminder of a grace
Not often poetry's
That, unresentful, hears

The music of what is.

Three score and ten

for Pearse Hutchinson

How you've survived, God knows,
Who were never one to use
dumb-bell and diet, or choose
prosperous avenues.
Asleep in Spain – cheap wine
dangled in your fine
white fingers, miraculous booze
unspilled at the angled brink –
you'd wake, we'd talk and drink
and talk, till now I think

my cradled telephone
could well have kept talking on,
so soon our conversation
is taken up again,
as though salt seas and tears,
years, whiter hairs,
powerless to intervene.
Shrugging, they recognise
no separations confuse
the steadily generous

of heart.
       Sometimes a group
is round you, but a gap
made always, stool pulled up,
and chill and years unwrap
their needless shawl, we all
feel warm, with you, and equal.
You, angered at the drop
of a hat or a word if you sense
one bullied, with no defence,
(and speedy to take offence

yourself. Why not? Your heart
is open, when others' are shut).
Wits, Sads, you admit,
and me, on a visit –
    oh, could you realise
    how it sets me up in my eyes
    as someone worthy of it! –
May I be so? May we soon
be talking not ten but nineteen
(and more than three-score) to the dozen,

with no one shouted down,
a space for each between.
(The best talkers listen.)
In the County Bar at Lucan
talking with you, I knew
there was nothing I'd rather do.
For me so rare a sensation
a man must stand up and admit it.
Nor will you doubt that.

Birthday thanks

addressed to Laurence Whitfield with whom I walked the River Severn, from estuary to source, and the River Wye from source to estuary. We did a portion each summer. It took us twenty years.

You won't stay sixty forever (after all,
it's taken thirty years to get there
since we first met) – so I hurry to celebrate
you and this day and the way we have walked the river,
from estuary to source, a fraction every summer,
with no cross words, crossed swords
(something to sing about, surely) that I remember.

What *do* I remember? I think I saw
most of what rolled in front of us hour by hour,
though Bewdley, Upton, Bridgnorth blur – and where
did the white-bearded mask of a fox from a coloured cave
look down on us both alone, always alone
until we hit the next town, limping? (By instinct
always at opening time?) You will remember,

it's lying reeled inside your sculptor's eye:
'That sandstone cliff by the ruined orchard. Remember?'
Both hands relate these places in the air,
put them together in their spatial order.
With a map you are like a musician reading a score,
though sometimes we're puzzled, then one or the other
ponders, points, 'There?' as if we remember

something, and so maybe deserved our angel on Plinlimmon
where we were lost, at the source, as he rose out of nowhere
an abrupt apparition with a halo of hair,
who impatiently turned us about in that featureless place
and improbably vanished, though not before snorting,
'*I* would have *begun* at the source!' So we did
and splashed through the mud of the birth of the other river

47

which you tripped headlong into, quietly sighing –
all the previous night your clothes on the heater drying –
my glasses so mud-splashed I couldn't see but I heard your
resigned exhalation, the sound of a tyre going flat.
You flinched when cows ran towards us, we had to detour.
'They'd stop if you turned to face them!' 'Do *they* know that?'
I find what I'm trying to honour is sheer good nature.

Llangurig, Clyro, Erwood, Bredwardine –
where I grabbed Kilvert's bedroom – Herefordshire,
you growing mutt-and-jeff, me increasingly four-eyes,
groaning louder each year at stiles we have to climb over...
What's friendship? 'A cheerful intelligent face
is the end of culture and the purpose of nature.'
A quote from American Emerson I remember

which suits you, and suited the voice I seemed to hear on
                                        Plinlimmon
(or was helped to remember) of new-born Sabrina
who giggles and wriggles, singing, through emerald mosses,
then is matronly, graceful; I told you, and you were respectful,
as you were when I'd wondered aloud, 'Was that an angel?'
though of such Hibernian fancies Mancunian-doubtful.
So, two rivers on, I am grateful, as I hope you'll believe and
                                        remember.

Thanks

for Kate

Of highest graces which
The soul of man can prove
Brief possession of,
Thanks and praise are best.

The poorest of us rich
With life, if little else.
Dignum et justum est.
Praise and thanks therefore.

They boom inside, a pulse,
Joy, we peer and stare,
Surprised to find it there,
And little understand.

There is one who here
Is praised for living kindness
Sharp as builders' sand
Which binds a house together,

Containment, also rescue,
And that one is you.
The glory and the strength is –
(I thank, therefore I am,

A joke you will endure
With patience if you can,
My genes are in the pun) –
The strength is in the story;

From dailiness, from years,
Emerges parity:
To you belongs the glory,
That not before the tomb

Now neither knows nor cares,
Neither gives a damn,
So long as the job is done,
Who has rescued whom.